THE COMMON-SENSE APPROACH TO DREAM INTERPRETATION

by

Sally A. Breslin

Dedicated to
Kevin Hilley and Harry Kozlowski
for all of their help and encouragement
throughout the years.

Dedicated to
Kevin Hilley and Harry Kozlowski
for all of their help and encouragement
throughout the years.

Introduction

Why are our dreams important? Because when we are awake, we can control what pops into our heads. If it is an unpleasant or disturbing thought, we have the power to ignore it and think of something else. However, when we are asleep, we no longer are in control of our thoughts. At that point, the subconscious mind essentially says, "Yay! Time to party! Time to let loose and flood this brain with everything its owner has suppressed all day!"

This basically means that dreams represent our true, unfiltered, uncensored thoughts and emotions.

By the time you finish reading this book, hopefully you will have the ability to more fully understand and interpret the meanings of your dreams. My method is simple and effective because I base my interpretations on common sense and word association. I use basic, everyday terms. And I promise that you won't find references to any dream "gurus" such as Freud or Jung.

I also must point out that I'm not a psychic, nor do I own a crystal ball. In fact, I do not believe dreams predict or forecast any future events...not unless the person having the dream happens to be clairvoyant. Dreams simply are a product of the dreamer's own mind, nothing more.

I can remember standing in the checkout line in a supermarket many years ago and seeing a rack of mini-books near the registers. One of the books was a dream dictionary that alphabetically listed the things people commonly dream about – animals, falling, kissing, rain, etc. – and their meanings.

I flipped open the book to the "G" page and saw "grasshoppers" listed. It said, "If you dream about grasshoppers, beware – all of your crops are going to die."

I couldn't help it, I burst out laughing (which caused the people in front of me in line to turn around and stare at me).

As I continued to flip through the pages of the book, it became clear to me not only how ridiculous some of the interpretations sounded, but also how they didn't apply to everyone. I realized that one size definitely did not fit all.

Take the grasshopper interpretation, for example. How would it apply to a person living in a small apartment in the middle of the city? Which crops would die? The aloe plant on the coffee table?

So that was how, back in the 1980s, I became interested in learning more – much more – about dreams and their meanings.

The information I gathered helped me to develop a more logical method of dream interpretation, mainly through basic trial and error. I constantly asked my friends and relatives about their dreams and soon, I came to realize I could tell exactly what was going on in their lives solely from their dreams. And when I gave them my interpretations, they acted as if I had some magical powers or ESP.

There was nothing magical about it. *They* were the ones who were telling me everything I needed to know about their current lives, thanks to their dreams.

My interpretations eventually led to an offer to write a weekly "dream" column for a chain of New England newspapers, which I did for over 30 years. I also interpreted dreams live, on the air, on numerous radio shows across the country, with a regular stint on Kevin Hilley's morning wake-up show on WJYY in Concord, NH. One of those radio shows was heard by a TV executive who contacted me to offer me a regular spot interpreting dreams on a major network's morning program. The catch – I would have to move to New York City. I politely declined.

Also, psychologists began to contact me to discuss their patients' dreams, which I thought was both amusing and flattering, considering I was nothing more than a self-taught interpreter.

At this point, I would like to emphasize that this book contains my own personal views and opinions about dreams, and perhaps some "experts" might not agree with my interpretations. But as I stated above, one size does not fit all.

So now I would like to share my methods with you…mainly because if you ever *do* dream about grasshoppers, I don't want you to spend a single minute worrying about your crops...or your aloe plant.

Facts and Misconceptions

First of all, I'd like to discuss a few observations and misconceptions about dreams.

I can't tell you how many people have said to me, "I *never* dream. The minute my head hits the pillow, I'm dead to the world."

The truth is, everyone dreams, but not everyone recalls doing so. In fact, the average is three to five dreams per night. Some people have even more, as many as eight to ten. You've probably noticed, however, that the dreams you most often remember are those that occur just as you are about to wake up. That's because you become more conscious of what is going on in your mind when you are closer to being awake.

I also often hear, "I never dream in color, I always dream in black and white."

People actually dream of things the way they see them in real life because the mind stores images the way they are seen. A person who is color-blind might have, understandably, dreams that lack certain colors, but if a person who has good eyesight and no physical problems says he or she dreams only in black and white, it usually means that is the way the dream was remembered, not how it truly was. It also can indicate that the dreamer might be going through a dark or gloomy period that is causing his or her mind to remember only the drab, colorless and gray areas of a dream.

Many people have told me they think dreams are nothing more than a bunch of nonsensical images that mean absolutely nothing, so trying to form any sort of rational interpretation based on them essentially is impossible.

I do realize that more often than not, dreams will seem totally absurd and make no sense whatsoever to the dreamer, but even the seemingly ridiculous dreams *do* have important meanings and messages.

Take, for example, a man who once approached me in the parking lot of a radio station after I'd just finished doing a live show.

"I just heard you on the air," he said to me. "And I think all of this dream-interpretation stuff is nothing but baloney! Dreams don't mean anything at all. They're just a bunch of crazy, random images."

I looked at him and asked, "Have *you* had any interesting dreams lately?"

"Yeah," he said, with a very deliberate smirk, obviously prepared to challenge me. "I had a dream that my wife was standing in a bucket of ice and holding a trout! Are you going to tell me there's some deep, hidden meaning to a ridiculous dream like that?"

"Is your wife a warm and loving woman?" I asked.

He shook his head. "Hell, no! She's a real cold fish!"

I smiled. "Congratulations. You just interpreted your own dream!"

One common misconception about dreams is that even though a dream might seem to last an hour, it's actually only a few seconds long in real life.

Dreams actually do occur in real time. If last night's dream feels as if it dragged on for 30 minutes, then it probably did. Contrary to popular belief, dreams don't flash by in a nanosecond. Also, the events, especially in the longer dreams, rarely unfold in chronological order. Think of the scenes in dreams as being similar to what you would see on a TV screen if you kept pressing the buttons on the remote control. So if the setting in the beginning of a dream is a movie theater at night, odds are that the majority of the rest of the dream will not take place there. Dreams tend to jump from one location and time of day or year to another, often several times per dream. So although a dream's location might start out in a movie theater on a summer night, it then might, during the course of the dream, switch to a barn, a shopping mall or a former classroom, and conclude in a forest in mid-winter. For this reason, whenever someone describes a lengthy dream to me and everything in it flows along in perfect sequence, I immediately suspect the person was doing more daydreaming (or fantasizing) than actual dreaming.

The remote-control comparison also is the reason why when you wake up in the middle of a beautiful dream and are eager to fall back to sleep so you can continue it, it rarely happens. Your mind's remote-control contains such a vast number of "stations," the odds of randomly finding the same one you previously were tuned into are extremely slim.

Another common misconception involves dreams about falling. More often than I can count, I have been asked if it's true that if you dream you are falling and don't wake up before you hit the ground, then you will die in real life and thus, never wake up.

Whenever I'm asked this question, I never fail to be amused. I always respond with, "That's impossible to answer...mainly because dead people can't tell anyone what they were dreaming about right before they died."

Actually, dreams about falling most commonly are associated with the dreamer's feelings of insecurity or a loss of control. If the dreamer does hit the ground in the dream, the intensity of the impact is what is important. The harder the landing, the more difficult the dreamer believes his or her real-life problem(s) will be to resolve.

Another thing that amuses me is when someone tells me, "My mother came to me in my dream and gave me some great advice," or "my ex-boyfriend sent me a message in my dream last night."

The truth is, if someone offers you advice in a dream, whatever is being said actually is nothing more than your own words to yourself. After all, the thoughts originate in and come from *your* mind, no one else's.

So if your great-grandmother appears in a dream and tells you not to take that new job on the other side of the country, it's actually *you* telling yourself not to take it because of your own doubts and fears – which you've probably been suppressing during your waking hours.

I also have discovered that most people are unable to dream about anything they actually wouldn't do in real life. One particular young woman immediately comes to mind. She was raised with extremely high morals and was determined to remain pure until her wedding night. Still, in preparation for the future "big event," she decided to educate herself on the subject by watching several "adult" movies and reading a lot of steamy romance-novels.

"In my dreams, I always meet these gorgeous men," she complained to me. "We start kissing and things get really passionate. But before anything can happen, I always wake up! It's *so* frustrating!"

"That's because your morals are so high, your subconscious won't allow you to go any farther in your dreams than you would allow yourself to go in real life," I told her.

So her determination to remain pure was verified in her dreams.

But there are other people whose dreams do not back up their real-life claims. I remember one man who appeared to be a staunch pacifist, preaching peace and love and claiming to be a true believer in "talking things out" and never, not *ever*, resorting to violence. Yet, his dreams constantly were filled with visions of himself harming people, picking fights in bars and shouting obscenities at strangers.

"Why am I dreaming that I'm doing such terrible things?" he asked me. "I would *never* do anything like that in real life!"

But his dreams were telling me otherwise. As I previously stated, when you're asleep the "real" you is free to come out. This man obviously was suppressing a lot of anger in his waking life, and it manifested itself in his dreams. Sure enough, I later heard he'd been arrested for domestic violence.

Another question I'm often asked is something similar to: "The other night I dreamed about my old college sweetheart, whom I haven't seen in 20 years. Why on earth would I, completely out of the blue like that, suddenly dream about him?"

The answer is simple. Triggers.

Triggers are so subtle, so sneaky, you don't even realize they're there. You could be walking through a

mall and the music playing in the background is a song
that often played when you were with a former
sweetheart. Or a sales clerk might be wearing the same
cologne your ex used to wear. One sniff of the cologne
and/or a few notes of a song are all your brain needs to
unlock a formerly "closed" file and make your sweetie
from the past suddenly appear, seemingly out of
nowhere, in your dream that night.

On a less romantic note, the guy in front of you at the
supermarket checkout might have gray hair and a
mustache just like your dentist's, and you'll end up
dreaming about Dr. Driller that evening. Then you'll
wake up scratching your head and wondering why on
earth you had a dream about your dentist.

There also are dreams that repeat themselves on a
regular basis. Although they aren't exact clones of each
other, they all will contain a similar theme. One of my
friends frequently dreamed about being lost, for
example. Another's dreams always contained
snowstorms.

Dreams recur because your subconscious is trying to
make you realize or figure out something, so it
essentially acts like a nagging friend or family member.
Until you are able to understand why a dream keeps
recurring, it's likely to continue to repeat itself (which is
all the more reason why it might be a good idea to learn
how to interpret your dreams).

I'm also very frequently asked about nightmares, the
disturbing side of dreams, especially when children have
them. Nightmares usually occur when something in real
life is frightening or worrying a person. These dreams
commonly involve being chased by something or
someone, which indicates a desire to get as far away
from a problem as possible instead of facing it and
attempting to resolve it. Children who are bullied at

school and are afraid to tell anyone about it, frequently experience nightmares.

Another common dream involves being naked. At least one out of every five people who ask me about dreams mentions being naked in them. These dreamers often seem embarrassed or ill at ease to broach the subject, probably because they fear it involves something sexual. Again, the interpretation is based on how the nakedness is presented in the dream. For example, if you dream you are walking naked into a party and you're not feeling shy or embarrassed, it indicates you are the type of person who doesn't hide behind a facade of any kind. You are comfortable with "revealing" your true self to everyone because you have nothing to conceal. But if you walk naked into that same party and feel a desperate need to run and hide because you're so humiliated, it means just the opposite. You are not comfortable with showing the "real you" to anyone.

However, if you dream you are passionately kissing your significant other or someone you have fantasized about being with, and then you remove all of your clothes and find yourself naked, well, that interpretation pretty much is self-explanatory.

While I'm on the subject of sensual dreams, some of them are not at all obvious until you consider the symbolism. I remember doing a live radio-show when a woman called to ask me why her 13-year-old son kept dreaming about telephone poles sliding in and out of tunnels. The DJ, whose show on which I was a guest at the time, later told me he wished he'd have taken a photo of my expression at that moment! All I could manage to say to the caller was, "Tell your son, 'welcome to puberty!'" I didn't dare elaborate any further.

And finally, I want to mention the all-too-common "bathroom" dream, where you're desperately searching for a bathroom but can't seem to find one anywhere.

All I can say is be glad you can't, because if you *do* find a place to "go" and start to relieve yourself in your dream, you just might wake up with a wet bed.

So if you're dreaming about urgently looking for a place to "go," my advice is to get up and head to the bathroom.

Quickly.

Colors

Colors are significant in dreams because most represent the dreamer's mood or current state of mind.

If a specific color stands out in a dream, it is important to understand why.

Take the color red, for example. Red can be associated with many different emotions. It can represent anger, such as in "seeing red." It can represent passion, as in "red hot," or embarrassment, as in "red-faced." It might signify a monetary loss, such as being "in the red" or "burned" in a bad business deal. It also can represent blood, especially if the dreamer has been emotionally "wounded" by someone he or she trusted. Red even might be associated with someone who is evil or demonic because devils often are depicted as being red in color or having glowing red eyes.

So, if a woman were to describe her dream as, "I dreamed I met this great-looking guy at a dance. When we started to dance, the lighting in the room switched to a glowing red color that kept getting brighter," more than likely the interpretation would indicate a growing passion between the man and woman.

But if that same woman said, "I was enjoying myself at a dance in my dream, when my scumbag of an ex-husband suddenly walked in. The lighting in the room turned a deep shade of red, growing deeper in color as he approached me," then the color red probably would represent anger.

Or if she described her dream as, "I was dancing some really fancy steps and everyone was watching me. Suddenly, I slipped on a wet spot on the floor and landed flat on my face. The dress I was wearing, which was beige, turned bright red."

In this situation, red could mean she either was embarrassed because she had fallen, or that she had injured herself in the fall and was bleeding – a symbol of being "wounded" emotionally.

Sometimes a color can signify emotions that are completely opposite of each other. The color blue is a good example. Blue can represent happiness, such as blue skies, blue heaven, or even the bluebird of happiness. But it also can indicate that the dreamer is depressed and suffering from a bad case of the "blues."

So once again, the analysis would depend entirely on how the color actually is used in the dream.

"I work as a painter," one dreamer told me. "And ever since my girlfriend, the woman I was certain was the love of my life, broke up with me, I have been dreaming I'm painting every wall in my building some shade of blue."

In this instance, the color blue obviously would represent feelings of depression, not happiness.

Blue also can indicate loyalty, such as being "true blue," which would not apply to the above dream, considering his girlfriend left him.

Green is another color that can be interpreted in many different ways. It can represent a desire for wealth because money is green. It can represent eagerness to raise a family or conceive a child because green is the color of most things that "grow" on earth. It can signify jealousy, as in being "green with envy" or the "green-eyed monster." It even can indicate feelings of nausea, such as when someone's complexion is described as looking a bit green.

And green can represent an inexperienced person, such as a "greenhorn."

Based on the descriptions above, how would you interpret the use of the color green in the following dream?

"I dreamt I was about to get married and the bridesmaids were wearing lovely, flowing gowns in various shades of green. My bouquet was adorned with green ribbons, and the wedding cake was decorated with green vines made of fondant."

If you are thinking that in this instance, the color green means the woman is eager to get married so she can start, or "grow." her family, you probably are correct.

Some colors are pretty much self-explanatory. Black, for example, is commonly associated with gloom and depression, or the "dark" side of something, while white is associated with purity, cleanliness and light, because it is the lightest color of all. On a deeper level, white also is the color of snow, so an excess amount of white items in a dream could represent someone who is feeling cold or emotionless. White also is associated with bleaching, which removes all color, making something look fresh and new, so it could represent a new or fresh start – a clean slate. Again, the way the color is used in the dream is what determines which definition most closely fits the situation.

Sometimes there can be more than one predominant color in a dream, such as in this high-school girl's dream:

"I had a dream I went shopping for my prom dress. My mother picked out a long, lacy white one for me, but I really fell in love with this bright-red short one with sequins on it. There also was another dress in black and white that I really liked, but had mixed feelings about. I woke up before I found out which dress I bought, if any."

The dreamer seems to be torn between staying "pure" on prom night, as she knows her mother would want her to do (which is why she dreamed her mother selected a white gown), or giving in to her passion and allowing things to get "hot" (which her personal choice of a red dress indicates). The sequins also suggest she really wants to "shine" and stand out on prom night. The fact that the dress of her choice was short, rather than a gown, represents a desire to be more daring and less conservative. The black and white dress indicates she is torn between her dark side and her good side – the proverbial good versus evil – concerning what she might be considering doing after the dance.

The reason why she awoke before a dress decision could be made was because she still was undecided about what to do on prom night. Her dream could not make that decision for her because, as I previously stated, dreams come from the dreamer's own mind, and her mind still was undecided and confused.

The following two dreams, both from male dreamers, have the color yellow in them, but their interpretations are vastly different:

"I dreamed I was meeting my girlfriend's family for the first time and was really nervous about it. I drove over to their house and just as I was walking up to the front door, the door suddenly changed from white to a dark yellow. It totally freaked me out."

And the second dream:

"I've been worried about some health issues lately and had a dream the other night that my doctor told me I was fine and probably would live to be 100. When I left the doctor's office and walked back out to my car, everything outside had a very bright, yellow glow."

In the first dream, the dreamer is feeling apprehensive about meeting his girlfriend's family for the first time. A door represents entering a new phase in one's life. In this case, the color yellow, especially a darker shade, indicates cowardice or fear, which stems from the old slang term, "yellow-bellied."

In the second dream, because the dreamer was so pleased and relieved to receive good news from his doctor, the color yellow when he stepped outside represents happiness and sunshine – feeling "golden" or as good as gold.

Of course, there are many more colors I haven't explained, but the ones above are a few examples that demonstrate how to use word association to figure out a specific color's meaning and significance in a dream.

Numbers

Numbers often play an important role in interpreting dreams, although there is no set-in-stone definition for each one. Again, a lot depends on how they are used in each individual dream.

The number one, for example, can represent feeling like a true winner or champion – reaching the top, as in, "We're number one!"

On the opposite side, however, it also can represent someone who is feeling lonely – unloved and alone. The song lyric, "One is the loneliest number," comes to mind.

And less often, the number one, especially when paired with a zero, as in the number 10, can be symbolic of a man and woman together, because the shape of the "1" represents the man's genitalia and the "0," the woman's. Taking that into consideration, the number 1001 then would represent two men and two women, or the number 110 would be two men and one woman.

The number two also can symbolize a couple, but unlike the one and zero together, which specifically are male and female, the number two can represent two men, two women and/or two children in any combination of sexes.

If a dreamer keeps seeing the number two in his or her dream, it can represent a longing to find a significant other and become a loving couple.

The number two also can indicate a pair of anything, such as shoes, bookends or even twin siblings. Or, it can represent a person who is two-faced or exhibits a split or dual personality.

Two can indicate receiving an unwanted or unsolicited opinion, as when someone puts in his or her "two cents' worth.".

And finally, but not as commonly, there is "number two" that represents a certain bodily function. If someone's dream sounds very negative and contains the number two, it could indicate experiencing a "crappy" (I am being polite here!) or unpleasant day.

The number three often has been associated with religion by many because they believe it is symbolic of the Father, the Son and the Holy Spirit. I, however, think of the number three as more of a family symbol – a couple with a child – therefore, three people.

The number three also can represent a dreamer who is feeling out of place or unwanted, such as in "three's a crowd." A love triangle, where two people are competing for the same person, also involves the number three.

The number four has many different meanings , but the most common refer to good luck (four-leaf clover), traveling or getting away (on four wheels), being old-fashioned or a "square" (four-sided), specific times of the year (four seasons), and animals or someone displaying animalistic behavior (four-legged).

The number five can represent a need for rest or relaxation (take five), anything to do with the hand, such as manual labor, stealing, or shaking someone's hand (five fingers), celebrating an achievement (high five), or something worthy of the highest praise or esteem (five-star rating)

The number six most commonly is associated with being physically fit (a six-pack), recreational drinking (also a six-pack), death or dying (six feet under), getting rid of or disposing of something (deep six), or pertaining to sex because the words "six" and "sex" sound so similar.

Now let's see how the number seven is used in the following dream, sent to me by a recent college graduate:

"A week ago I applied for a very prestigious job and am waiting to hear back from the personnel manager. Last night, I dreamed he called me and said, 'Young man, I am calling to inform you I have decided to hire you. Your employee number will be seven, so please don't forget it.' I remember not feeling as happy or as excited about being hired as I'd thought I would. And why did I dream about the number seven? I don't understand its significance."

Most commonly, the number seven represents either the seven days of the week or "lucky seven," indicating good fortune. The key to interpreting its significance in this particular dream is the dreamer's mood. He said he really did not feel happy about getting the job, so it doesn't sound as if he is feeling very lucky or is in "seventh heaven." Therefore, I suspect the number seven in this case reveals the dreamer's fears that the job is going to involve a lot of hard work, perhaps often seven days a week, which obviously doesn't appeal to him.

The number seven also can represent the seven deadly sins, but this dream does not contain enough detail to determine if one of the sins might apply here. If the dreamer had said the personnel manager was seated at his desk with his feet up on it, and was eating a large pizza and spilling it all over his shirt during the interview, then one of the deadly sins, such as "gluttony," might apply.

Not very frequently, the number seven can represent restlessness. This stems from the old expression "seven-year itch," which was rumored to be the point in a relationship or marriage when one member of the couple begins to experience boredom and goes searching for a more exciting partner.

The number eight can indicate a difficult or bad situation, which is derived from the expression "behind the eight-ball." It also can be symbolic of infinity, something that lasts forever, because the figure eight has no beginning or end, and when turned on its side, it forms the infinity symbol.

And sometimes the number eight can represent "ate" because the words sound alike.

How would you interpret the number nine in this dream?

"I dreamt I was getting married and had nine bridesmaids, nine groomsmen and was married on Sept. 9th. In real life, I'm not even engaged or in a serious relationship. But I can't wait to find my Mr.

Right and get married...and then start a family soon after that."

The number nine seems to be all this dream is about. Even the month of September is the ninth month. I clearly can see two interpretations here. First, "cloud nine" comes to mind because of how happy I'm certain this woman will be when she does find her Prince Charming and her wedding day finally arrives. And then, she will be eager for the nine months of pregnancy to begin, when she starts her family.

Nine also can represent putting your everything into something, as in "the whole nine yards." I do believe this woman is putting all of her efforts into finding her Mr. Right.

The number ten, as previously mentioned, can be symbolic of a male and a female, usually a couple. Ten also can represent a couple holding hands, because the two hands have a total of 10 fingers.

On the subject of hands, the number 10 can symbolize an artisitc person such as a sculptor or potter, who uses his or her hands (all ten fingers) to form or mold their creations.

I could write an entire book on numbers alone because there are so many variations, but hopefully, this will give you an idea. As I previously have emphasized, their interpretation depends solely on the way in which they are used in the dream.

Emotions and Decisions

I always have believed that the quickest way to learn how to do something is to use the hands-on approach and learn by doing. So I have selected some of the dreams that have been sent to me throughout the years and together, we will interpret them.

This first collection of dreams deals with feelings, emotions and even some major decisions.

1. "In my dream, I was shopping for new furniture for my house, and everything I picked out was really hideous-looking and ugly. Most of it looked as if someone had already used it and tossed it out, yet I seemed willing to pay good money for it."

Peggy

First of all, we have to judge the general tone of this dream. Does Peggy sound happy? Distressed? Confused?

Secondly, in dreams, a house most often represents the dreamer's own body, which stems from the old saying, "my body is my temple."

Therefore, it would appear that at the time of Peggy's dream, she was feeling down on herself and her appearance, and considered herself undeserving of nice things (her statement that everything she picked out was hideous-looking and ugly indicates this), otherwise she would have selected new, attractive items. Money did not seem to be a problem because she mentioned spending it freely.

So although Peggy appears to think she could use a new look or makeover and reinvent herself, her dream indicates she currently has a "why even bother?" defeatist attitude.

2. "I had a dream that my wall clock was really slow. I put in a fresh battery, but it still kept getting slower every hour. So I bought a new clock and it turned out to be even worse."

Christopher

There is an old saying that time flies when you're having fun. Christopher's time, however, appears to be dragging by in this dream.

I see two possible reasons for this. First of all, prior to his dream, he could have been experiencing feelings of uselessness because everything he'd been doing had turned out to be unproductive and a waste of time. Time going by too slowly also can represent boredom and clock-watching, especially at work.

Installing a fresh battery suggests he at least wants to make an effort to improve his life, but thus far, he hasn't expended much "energy" doing so.

Either way, I think Christopher really could benefit from adding some excitement and adventure to his life.

3. "Lately I have been having a recurring dream and can't understand why. It's not exactly the same every time, but each dream is very similar. In it, I'm usually trying to walk in five-inch high-heels. I am very unsteady in them and my legs look and feel like rubber with every step. Another night, I dreamed I tried to walk in really high platform shoes, and I didn't have any luck with those, either. Any idea why?"

Maddy

Usually when people attempt to gain height in a dream – either by climbing a ladder, standing on a chair, wearing higher shoes, etc. – it represents a desire to have people look up to them.

Maddy seems to be searching for respect, but her inability to walk in higher heels indicates something is "off balance" in her life and is making her feel weak and vulnerable instead of strong and sure-footed. She also seems to think she might be setting herself up for a big fall.

The fact there was no one in her dream to lean on or give her support when she was unsteady, represents a desire to learn how to stand up for herself and for what she believes in, no matter how difficult. Her dream is a recurring one because she is putting pressure on herself to succeed, but thus far, hasn't convinced herself she is capable of doing so.

4. "I'm wondering why I've recently had two dreams in which I'm suffering from a terrible backache, to the point where I'm walking all

hunched over and can't even straighten up. In real life, I don't suffer from any back pain at all and am very active in sports."

Nathan

So what would make an apparently healthy man dream he is suffering from terrible back pain? In real life, most backaches occur when someone tries to lift heavy items or overdoes an activity. The key in this dream is Nathan's hunched-over position. This leads me to suspect that in real life, he is carrying a heavy burden (emotional), as if the weight of the world were on his shoulders. The most common reason for such a dream is a concern about finances.

5. "I had a dream that I went to visit my daughter and her husband and they told me they were expecting my first grandchild. When I got home, I went to take off my makeup, and when I looked at myself in the mirror, I was shocked to see that all of my teeth were missing!"

Vivian

There are two times in people's lives when they have no teeth – when they are babies and often when they are elderly. I noticed that nowhere in Vivian's description of her dream did she say she was excited over the prospect of becoming a grandmother. I suspect, because of her toothless reflection in the mirror, it's because she's afraid that being called "Grandma" will make her feel too old. She also mentioned removing her makeup at home. This means she feels she can be her "natural" self (and not conceal her emotions) only when she is alone.

25

This dream doesn't mean she's actually going to become a grandmother in real life. It means she is dreading growing old too soon.

6. "In my dreams lately, I never seem to be able to find my car after I've parked it somewhere, usually in parking lots at schools, for some reason. I always wake up before I find it."

Rick

Vehicles in dreams most often are symbolic of the dreamer's "drive" or ambition in life. Rick seems to have lost his motivation to move forward. He said he usually parks his car in school parking-lots, so this suggests he feels he still has a lot to learn about something in particular, but for some reason, doesn't have the incentive to do so. The fact that this is a recurring dream indicates he considers his current situation to have no immediate or obvious solution.

7. "I was wondering if you could shed some light on what this dream means. In it, I was standing on a street corner, waiting to cross the street. Every time the street looked clear and I stepped off the curb, cars and trucks would come zooming up out of nowhere and nearly run me over, so I had to jump back. I never did get across."

Matt

Crossing a street (or a bridge) is symbolic of crossing over into a new aspect or phase of life, so Matt apparently has been contemplating making some changes. However, because he never was able to get any farther than a few inches from the curb, it indicates he is hesitant to take any big steps forward at the present time.

I suspect, due to the fact that when a person steps off a curb, it's usually into a gutter, that he currently feels as though he is in a rut – doing the same thing day after day. But this is what he is familiar with and what he does best. Therefore, making a change is difficult for him. The traffic zooming up and nearly hitting him tells me he is afraid to too hastily make any decisions concerning his future because he could end up "falling flat" on his face.

8. "Why do I keep dreaming I'm being sick to my stomach? In real life, I feel just fine and have a great appetite."

Nathan

Vomiting is the body's way of getting rid of something that is toxic or difficult to digest. Therefore, something obviously has been "eating away" at Nathan and he wants to purge himself of whatever it is.

This type of dream usually is associated with a guilty conscience and a desire to come clean about it. Until Nathan opens up and confesses the truth to someone, his dreams about vomiting are likely to continue.

9. "I dreamed that I bought a new dress and my husband asked me to model it for him. I did, and as I was posing in the dress, I noticed that the skin on my arms nearly had become transparent! I could see my veins and even the blood flowing through them. It was scary."

Lorraine

The expression "thin-skinned," which the dictionary defines as being overly sensitive to criticism and insults, immediately comes to mind. Lorraine seems to fear her husband's opinion of her because she obviously lacks self-confidence. The longer she posed for him, the thinner her skin became. She also used the word "scary" to describe her dream, which leads me to suspect that her husband tends to be brutally honest when giving his opinion, even if it is hurtful.

10. "I dreamed that I was in a national spelling bee, standing in front of a huge audience. I spelled just about every word wrong, yet I wasn't eliminated, for some reason. Everyone else who misspelled a word was immediately dismissed, however."

Rob

Spelling is associated with a strong knowledge of words. Rob's dream indicates he has the tendency to blurt out things before really thinking about them, so they often come out the "wrong" way. But he also seems to have a knack for talking his way out of whatever was said, so he still ends up looking like a winner.

11. "I had a dream that my mother knitted sweaters for my dad, my older brother and me. All of the sweaters were solid pink in color and a little tight when we tried them on. In real life, my mother doesn't even know the first thing about knitting."

Isaac

The color pink usually is a happy color because of an expression that dates centuries back: feeling "in the pink," which indicates the peak of good health and spirits. Knitting, in this particular dream, especially since the sweaters were a bit tight, sounds as if it represents a "close-knit" family. So I would say that Isaac comes from a happy, well-adjusted family in which he, his parents and sibling all enjoy doing things together. He seems to credit his mother for keeping everything running smoothly.

If the sweaters in this dream had been a different color, however, such as black, which represents gloom and depression, then the meaning would be different. Instead of a happy, close-knit family, it would indicate Isaac is not enjoying all of this "togetherness" and is craving some time to himself.

12. "My mother moved down to Florida last year, but when I dream about her, she usually is either moving into my basement, buying the house next door to me, or is renting an apartment on the next block."

Stacy

I sense that Stacy really misses her mother because in her dreams, the woman always is somewhere nearby rather than in Florida. Stacy's mother really seems to be "near and dear" to her heart.

However, because there is no indication of Stacy's mood in this dream, such as if she feels happy about her mother moving into her basement or buying the house next door, then it's also possible Stacy might be feeling that even though her mother has moved away, she still has a way of insinuating herself into her life, either by frequently calling or texting, asking too many questions (a.k.a being nosy) or constantly providing unwanted advice.

13. "Why do I keep dreaming about goats? They usually are running rampant through my house or following me everywhere, even to work. I was born and raised in the city and have never been around goats, nor do I have any interest in them."

Marcie

Goats actually can have several different meanings in dreams. I suspect that in Marcie's instance, however, because of the "running rampant" description, the goats represent human "kids" who are making her feel stressed in real life.

They also can represent someone, such as a boss or a co-worker, who is irritating and really "gets her goat." Or they can be symbolic of aging, such as becoming an "old goat."

While on the subject of animals in dreams, I must point out that they always represent human acquaintances of the dreamer. But before being able to interpret what they symbolize, the person's personality and mannerisms must be taken into consideration. For example, a dream about a pig could represent a friend who is a sloppy housekeeper, or who has terrible table manners, eats too much, or infrequently bathes. It even could represent someone who snorts when he or she laughs – or sleeps.

A wolf might be symbolic of someone who's a flirt ("That guy is such a wolf!"), someone who is sneaky (a wolf in sheep's clothing), or a ravenous eater ("He really wolfed down his food!").

So basically, in dreams, each animal's different characteristics usually can be applied in some way to a human's personality in the dreamer's life.

30

14. "I have been having dreams about my upcoming college class-reunion. In the dream, I walk into the room and everyone is dressed very formally in tuxedos and gowns. I, however, am wearing a plain white shirt and baggy jeans, with my hair not even combed. Everyone turns to look at me and I immediately feel embarrassed and run out. The strange thing is that in real life, I was very popular in college and always was the life of the party."

Roger

Although he might have been popular in college, I get the feeling Roger didn't stay in touch with his former classmates over the years, and now he is concerned they might not have much in common any more. The attire of his friends in his dream leads me to suspect he thinks most of them are well-off and successful, while he's just living more on the "comfortable" side.

The fact that he ran out of the reunion in his dream instead of staying to catch up with all of the news about his former classmates, indicates he really doesn't care to know what they've been doing since their college days... especially if they have been more successful than he has.

15. "I dreamed I went swimming with my older brother, Rick (we're both adults). We decided to swim out to a big rock about 400 feet from the shore. I made it to the rock and climbed onto it, but when I turned around to see where Rick was, I noticed he was struggling and was starting to sink. I don't know why, but I hesitated before I jumped back into the water to go help him."

Dylan

Even though Dylan's brother is older than he is, I get the impression Rick constantly needs Dylan's help to keep him "afloat." Rick's struggle to swim out to the rock indicates he probably is experiencing financial problems or is "drowning" in debt. I suspect that Rick has borrowed money from his brother on more than one occasion to help him keep his head above water, so to speak.

Dylan's dream clearly expresses his growing frustration with Rick's dependence on him for help, otherwise he wouldn't have hesitated before jumping back into the water to go to his aid.

16. "I had a very vivid dream that my teenage son's room was full of ants. In case you're thinking he's sloppy or messy, he actually keeps his room really neat for someone his age, so I'm puzzled."

Jeanne

Insects usually are symbolic of someone or something that is "bugging" or bothering the dreamer. So apparently Jeanne's son recently has been doing something that is a source of aggravation to her, for some reason.

17. "In my dream, I came home from work to discover that my house was being remodeled. There were workmen everywhere, sawing, hammering, painting and wallpapering. I stood there stunned because I hadn't called anyone to remodel anything."

Dianne

In dreams, a house represents the dreamer's own body. The windows are the eyes, the upper floor or attic is the brain, and the basement is the subconscious. So it would appear that Dianne has been feeling in need of a personal makeover. This could be something cosmetic, such as a new hairstyle or wardrobe, or something more complex, such as ending a current relationship or switching careers.

18. "I was wondering what my dream means because I have had it more than once recently. In it, I am in a place that looks like I'd imagine heaven would look. There are clouds and angels and even harps. I seem at peace there until one of the angels comes over to me and says, 'You don't belong here! Go back to where you came from!' That's when I usually wake up. Even though I am in excellent health, I'm concerned this dream means I'm about to die."

Collin

As I said previously, I don't believe that dreams predict anything unless the person having the dream is a genuine clairvoyant, so Collin should not be concerned yet about purchasing his headstone.

If, however, he had specified he indeed is ill in real life, especially with something serious, like cancer, his dream then would suggest he's a fighter and is not prepared to give up and die – which is why the angel told him to leave.

But in this particular dream, because heaven represents a place where the "good" go, I suspect that for some reason, Collin doesn't consider himself to be a very respectable person at the present time. It could be because he is feeling guilty about something he's recently said or done. And although he would like to surround himself with kind, virtuous people, he is convinced he doesn't deserve to be in their company any time soon.

19. "I had a dream it was Christmas Eve and I came downstairs for a drink of water and saw Santa Claus putting gifts underneath the tree. Instead of being pleased, I grabbed a vase from the coffee table and smashed him over the head with it. Then when he fell down, I kicked him. I have no idea why I would dream of myself being so cruel, so I'm hoping you can explain why."

Heather

I have the feeling that Scrooge has nothing over on Heather when it comes to a "bah humbug!" attitude about Christmas. Beating up a popular symbol of Christmas suggests she is feeling severely stressed by all of the pressures associated with the holiday season.

Also, because Santa is symbolic of the gift-giving aspect of Christmas, she probably has become disenchanted due to all of the commercialism, and resents having to spend money on things she really can't afford.

She obviously is eager to get the holidays over and done with as soon as possible.

20. "I dreamed that my mother was the captain of my cheerleading squad at school! She showed up wearing a cheerleader outfit just like mine, short skirt and all, and was carrying a megaphone. I didn't feel at all embarrassed, however. I actually was pleased to see her!"

Cassie

Cassie's mother apparently is one of her biggest supporters, especially when it comes to school activities. Whatever Cassie does, or whatever decisions she makes, her mother tries to cheer her on rather than discourage her. Cassie seems to think of her mother as someone who can lift her spirits and her morale when she is feeling down or stressed. She also considers her mother to be more of a friend than an authoritative figure.

Relationships

This collection of dreams pertains to all types of relationships – romantic, family-oriented and "just friends."

1. "My boyfriend recently suggested that we move in together. That same night, I dreamed I was at his house and decided his front lawn looked too plain, so I bought two nice-looking trees and planted them. As soon as I did, a big wind came along and the trees toppled over. I re-planted them, but the same thing happened all over again."

Irene

Irene obviously isn't ready to move in with her boyfriend. The two trees represent the "growth" of two people together. Her trees kept falling over, however, which indicates she's not ready to put down permanent "roots" with this particular guy. And wind represents a relationship that has had to endure some turbulence, especially when it's a strong wind like the one in this dream.

Irene used the word "plain" to describe her boyfriend's lawn, which also could be symbolic of her feelings about him – basically dull and unexciting.

Her subconscious is telling her she should not rush into anything and therefore should not move in with him yet (if ever!). Hopefully, she will heed that advice.

2. "I had a dream that I called one of my ex-girlfriends and asked her how she was doing. She said she'd moved to Alaska. I asked her if she was still single, and she said, "Yes, and living very comfortably here in an igloo." Does this make any sense?"

Jay

Actually, it does. Did you notice that Jay seemed to associate everything cold and icy (Alaska, an igloo) with his ex-girlfriend? Although he's obviously still interested in her and would like to rekindle their romance (otherwise he wouldn't have asked her if she still was single), he doesn't hold much hope that she'll ever warm up to him again.

I get the impression she was the one who ended their relationship and he's finding it difficult to accept the fact that it's over.

3. "In my dream, I was floating over all of the houses in my neighborhood. My husband was on the ground shouting up at me to come back down before I hurt myself, but I ignored him and just kept floating. It was such a wonderful feeling, I hated to wake up."

Hayley

In this particular dream, floating appears to be symbolic of Hayley's desire to rise above all of her problems and get away from anything that is weighing her down. The fact she was in no hurry to come back when her husband called to her indicates she wants to enjoy the feeling of being totally free for a while (especially from him!).

4. "In my dream, I was walking with my longtime boyfriend. We hiked to the top of a hill and the scenery was breathtaking. He turned to kiss me and just as he did, I lost my footing, slipped and fell, rolling all the way down to the bottom of the hill. I remember just lying there, but I can't remember whether I was hurt or not."

Ramona

When it comes to romance, Ramona seems to think her current relationship rapidly is going downhill. There she was, essentially on top of the world and about to receive a romantic kiss, and instead ended up lying all alone at the bottom. To get back to her boyfriend would have involved a struggle, an uphill climb. This indicates the relationship currently has been requiring more and more effort to make it work.

Ramona mentioned he was her "longtime" boyfriend, which could be part of the problem. Perhaps she thinks his actions have become too routine and predictable, especially where passion (or lack thereof) is concerned.

5. "I recently have been dating a guy who's in one of my classes at college. So far, everything has been great and we are having a lot of fun together. But for some reason, this past week I have been dreaming that he takes me out only to very dimly lit places, like candlelight restaurants and dark clubs. In real life, we have a lot of dates in public, out in the bright sunlight, so this doesn't make sense."

Beth

Often a dream such as this one indicates the dreamer feels as if her boyfriend is embarrassed about being seen with her in public, so he takes her only to dark or secluded places, which is common when an affair is involved. Beth, however, states that she and her new boyfriend openly have been dating in public.

Therefore, I think her dream means she suspects he is hiding something about himself from her. Keeping her "in the dark" prevents her from "seeing the light" about his true character. The fact this dream keeps recurring indicates Beth already is having concerns about their relationship and is doubting the possibility of a long-term future with this guy.

6. "In my dream, it was my boyfriend's birthday so I went to the mall to look for a gift for him. In every men's clothing store, I bought him a necktie in a different color and pattern until I had a huge shopping bag full of them. The strange thing is that

my boyfriend never wears neckties and has no reason to.”

Georgia

Men often refer to neckties as "nooses" or "tourniquets," both of which tend to cut off their circulation. I get the impression Georgia is hoping for a lasting commitment from her boyfriend, perhaps even a marriage proposal. As corny as it may sound, she seems eager to "tie" the knot.

7. "I have had this dream twice in the past week. I'm locked inside a jail cell and my fiancé comes to visit me. He then tells me he's managed to find the key to the cell. I get all excited and tell him to hurry up and open the door and let me out. He smiles, says he'll have to think about it and then walks off and leaves me in there! He never unlocked the door in either of my dreams!"

Karen

It's pretty obvious that in real life, Karen's fiancé enjoys being in control. The fact she's in a jail cell represents feelings of being trapped and losing her freedom. She also seems to think her fiancé's decisions and actions are what hold the "key" to her future happiness.

In her dream, she is eager for him to release her from prison, which leads me to suspect she has been considering ending their relationship and being free once again, but he's not giving her any opportunity to discuss it with him. The fact that he smiled before walking off indicates she doesn't think he takes much of what she says seriously anyway. Unfortunately Karen's dreams

40

will continue to recur until she makes a firm decision about whether to marry this man or to break off their engagement.

8. "In my dream, I walked over to my boyfriend's house after school, the way I often do in real life. He lives only two blocks away from me, yet in my dream, I walked for blocks and blocks and still didn't reach his house. I woke up without ever getting there."

Anna

This dream tells me that Anna's relationship with her boyfriend isn't as close or as warm as it used to be. In fact, she apparently has been feeling there is a growing distance between them. She kept walking in the dream, however, determined to reach her boyfriend's house, even though she probably was feeling tired and frustrated. This indicates that despite her boyfriend's growing aloofness, she still is determined to try to make their relationship work.

9. "I have a crush on my boss, but he has no idea I do. The other night I dreamed he finally asked me out on a date. We had a nice time, but at the end of the evening, when he walked me to my door, I was anticipating a kiss. Instead, he suddenly sprouted vampire fangs and bit me on the neck! I really am curious to find out what this means."

Chloe

A vampire is symbolic of someone who will leave another person feeling physically and emotionally "drained." So even though Chloe has a crush on her boss and is fantasizing about having a romantic date with him, both her common sense and her subconscious are telling her not to pursue a relationship with him...other than one that is strictly business.

10. "I'm interested to know what my dream means. In it, I was at my boyfriend's house and for some reason, he was having trouble putting on his running shoes. No matter how hard he tried, he couldn't get them on his feet. I offered to help him, but he said no."

Lisa

I think it's significant that Lisa's boyfriend was trying to put on his "running" shoes. Lisa appears to suspect he might be thinking about leaving her but he has been "struggling" with making a decision.

She seemed eager to offer her assistance and help him speed up the process, however, so I sense she probably shares his feelings.

I also think that because he flatly refused her help, this indicates she prefers to allow him to be the one who finally ends their relationship.

11. "I dreamed I was at the mall with my wife and we were shopping for a new suit for me. Every suit I tried on that I thought looked good, she said she didn't like. She then picked out a suit and said, "Now this is what you need!" But when I tried it on, it was huge. In fact, it was so huge, another person could have fit into it with me. She, however, kept insisting it was just perfect, so I bought it."

Craig

Rather than stick with the suit he wanted, Craig bowed down to his wife and allowed her to choose one for him, probably to avoid a disagreement. This indicates that his wife usually makes the major decisions in the family. The fact that the suit she selected for him was too big means she frequently has a way of making him feel small or like less of a man in front of others.

12. "I had a dream that my new boyfriend suggested we go ice skating. We were having a nice time skating around together, arm in arm, when all of a sudden my skate blade got stuck in a crack in the ice and I fell. The fall woke me up."

Amy

This dream suggests that just when Amy begins to feel as if things are gliding along smoothly in a relationship, something inevitably happens to cause it to take a nosedive. As a result, she now lacks confidence and optimism whenever she starts dating someone new. She apparently has convinced herself that every relationship will end up causing her to be hurt in some way.

13. "In my dream, I was on a baseball team that was all women. Every time I was up at bat, I swung at every ball that was pitched to me and missed. No matter how positive I was that I could hit it, I never even managed to come close. I finally flung the bat on the ground and walked off the field."

Eric

Eric seems to be on a losing streak when it comes to women. Baseball terms such as "striking out" or not getting to "first base," could be symbolic of his recent dating history. Perhaps it's time for him to analyze what he's doing wrong and make a sincere effort to improve his batting average.

14. "I dreamt I was out in the woods, hunting. I'm not sure what I was hunting for, whether it was deer, turkey, or something else, but I was carrying a rifle and sneaking around. Suddenly, something moved in the bushes and I shot at it, without even seeing what it was. I rushed over to check things out and was shocked to see it was my wedding planner! I tried to revive her, but I couldn't. When I laughingly told my fiancée about my dream the next day, she wasn't amused at all, so I really need your help on this one!"

Brandon

Sorry to say, I don't think my interpretation is going to help Brandon's situation with his fiancée. First of all, hunting indicates he's still searching for something he feels is missing from his life. He mentioned sneaking around, so perhaps he already is doing something behind his fiancée's back.

He's also the type who seems to enjoy the thrill of a chase, so perhaps now that he's "captured" his fiancée's heart, he is feeling bored or restless.

Killing his wedding planner, even accidentally, suggests he is harboring some hostility toward her. Deep inside, he might be wishing he could put an abrupt end to all of the wedding planning and somehow make her, and everything else associated with the event, just disappear from his life.

To be honest, this dream pretty clearly tells me that Brandon is not ready to settle down and get married.

15. "I dreamed I was at a fair and there was a psychic reader there, so I had her tell my fortune. She told me I would soon meet the man of my dreams and we would get married, have two children and live a long, happy life together. I woke up feeling very positive and optimistic about my future. Do you think my dream means it actually will happen? Please say yes!"

Yvonne

As I mentioned previously, dreamers must understand that no matter who is speaking to them in their dreams, whether it's a fortuneteller or the Queen of England, all of the words actually are coming from their own minds. So in this dream, the psychic reader actually is Yvonne making the predictions and giving them to herself. Therefore, her dream is more wishful thinking than something prophetic. But if she is determined to make everything that was predicted come true and find the man of her dreams, there always is the possibility her dream just might motivate her to try a little harder to make it happen.

16. "I'm about to enter my first year of college, and recently had a dream about my mother. In it, she said she'd help me move into my dorm, but when it came time for me to leave home, my mother took out a long piece of rope and tied me up with it!"

Corrina

Corrina seems to be experiencing guilt about leaving home because she's concerned her mother is going to suffer from empty-nest syndrome and be depressed.

Rope can be interpreted as the "ties" that bind, or even an umbilical cord, symbolizing a permanent attachment to her mother. Guilt or no guilt, however, Corrina knows the time has come to finally cut the cord.

17. "I had a dream that I was out on a date with this really cute guy and everywhere we went, my parents were there! They were in the row behind us at the movies, then at the table next to us in the restaurant. And when my date drove me home, my parents pulled in right behind his car and just sat there."

Hannah

I get the feeling Hannah is young and perhaps has just started dating. Whenever she goes out, her parents' advice is so strongly embedded in her mind, she feels as if they are right there with her.

Her dream indicates she respects her parents and tries to live up to their expectations. Therefore, even when they aren't with her, she still tries to act the same way she would if they were. And if she did end up doing something she felt would not meet their approval, her conscience definitely would bother her.

18. "I had a dream that my ex-husband called to tell me he had a terminal illness and wanted to apologize for all the wrong he'd done to me so he could die in peace. I told him I could never forgive him and I'd be glad when he died because then I'd never have to see him again. I was surprised at how mean I was to him in the dream."

Amelia

It's obvious that Amelia still is harboring a lot of resentment toward her ex-husband, possibly because the divorce recently was finalized. She apparently feels that no matter how much he apologizes, he never will be able to make up for what he has done to her.

Wanting him dead in her dream doesn't necessarily mean she'd like to see him six feet under. More than likely it means she wants to put the marriage and divorce behind her because they are a "dead" issue. Although she seems ready to make a fresh start, she is finding it difficult to do so. As more time passes, however, it should become easier for her to completely let go.

19. "I dreamed that my aunt died, and her second husband and I began to date and talk about marriage. This man has been my uncle, though not blood-related, for most of my life and not once have I ever thought of him in a romantic way."

Kathryn

So has Kathryn been harboring a secret crush on her aunt's second husband all these years? The answer is no. This particular dream indicates that many of the qualities Kathryn admires in her uncle are qualities she would like her own man (or future husband) to have. In other words, she sees him as somewhat of a role model as far as husband material is concerned.

The fact that Kathryn dreamed her aunt was dead, however (barring the fact the woman currently is in poor health), could mean the two women have become distant over the years and their former closeness now seems to be fading.

20. "In my dream, I was dating this girl at school I think is really hot (she's the captain of the cheerleaders). But no matter where we went together, she wore these big old-fashioned headphones and listened to music."

Jason

Jason might have a crush on this cheerleader, but deep inside he believes he doesn't stand a chance of actually ever going out with her in real life. The cheerleader's headphones, which would block out all of the sounds around her, indicate Jason feels she's really not interested in hearing anything he might have to say.

21. "I had a dream that I went to a fireworks display with my girlfriend and the fireworks turned out to be mostly duds. Everyone there was complaining about how disappointed they were and how they should have stayed home. I had to agree with them."

Alan

I hate to say it, but Alan's dream tells me he is beginning to feel as if there no longer are any "sparks" or thrills in his relationship with his girlfriend. People who watch fireworks usually "ooh!" and "aah!" throughout the display, but the people in his dream seemingly were as unimpressed as he was. This tells me that other people in Alan's life also are beginning to notice how lackluster his relationship with his girlfriend has become. It's time for him to either make an effort to add more color and excitement to the relationship...or to move on.

**22. "My dream was both exciting and disturbing.
There is this really great-looking customer who often
comes into the store where I work and I am really
attracted to him. The other night, I dreamed we were
out on a date at a restaurant when he suddenly burst
out laughing for no apparent reason. I asked him
what was so funny, but he just continued to laugh
until everyone around us began to stare."**

Becky

Becky's subconscious is trying to tell her what she
already knows – that a relationship with this guy never
would work.

His laughing could indicate she thinks he never would
date someone like her and would think it was a big joke
if she ever got up the courage to invite him somewhere.
Either that, or she has observed, when he's come into
the store where she works, that she doesn't share his
strange sense of humor.

I noticed she mentioned only his good looks as the
reason why she's attracted to him. She says nothing
about him being a nice guy or sociable, etc.

So crush or no crush, she seriously should listen to
her subconscious.

**23. "I had a nightmare that my sister was killed in
a terrible car accident. The car that crashed into hers
turned out to be my boyfriend's, and he was the one
who was driving at the time. I remember thinking
that I couldn't possibly be with a man who caused
my sister's death. The dream left me really shaken
and I woke up crying so hard, my pillow was soaking
wet."**

Mindy

Mindy's boyfriend and her sister apparently have had some verbal "clashes" in real life that have caused Mindy to have some serious doubts about her relationship and possible future with this man.

Mindy seems to be anticipating a big blow-up between her boyfriend and her sister at some point in the near future, which will force her to have to decide whose side to take.

The fact that her sister died in her dream indicates Mindy is feeling as if her boyfriend is destroying her formerly close relationship with her sister, to the point where the two of them eventually might become estranged.

The reason why Mindy woke up crying is because she tends to suppress and conceal her true feelings during her waking hours. When she is asleep, however, she no longer has any control, so her tears are free to flow.

24. "In my dream, I was with my friend Nancy at a public swimming pool. This really handsome guy came along and invited us to dive off the high board with him. I told him I was afraid of heights, but Nancy went right up there with him and dove off the board, even though she'd never done it before. She hit her head on the bottom of the pool and was knocked out. I woke up not knowing if she was OK or not."

Kelly

Kelly seems to think that her friend Nancy takes too many risks, especially when it comes to members of the opposite sex. Too often she "plunges" right into a new relationship, getting way in over her head before she even knows what hit her. Inevitably, she ends up getting hurt.

Kelly, on the other hand, considers herself to be much more levelheaded and definitely more cautious.

25. "I had a dream that my boyfriend and I were on a carousel ride. Instead of being on horses that were side by side, he was on one that was about three horses ahead of mine. The ride seemed to go on and on, as if it never would end."

Kendra

Considering the motion of carousel horses, it appears that Kendra's relationship with her boyfriend currently is experiencing some ups and downs.

Her dream, because he was riding far ahead of her, indicates that one of their main problems is he considers himself to be the leader rather than an equal partner in their relationship. He also tends to make her feel as if she is going around in circles and getting nowhere with him.

26. "The other night I dreamed that two of my friends and I went to a diet group meeting. Afterwards, we went to a candy-making class where we learned how to make caramels. In real life, my friends and I are not overweight, so I'm really curious about this dream."

Debbie

The caramels lead me to believe that Debbie and her friends really "stick" together, especially during times of need. And I suspect the diet group is symbolic of them being with each other "through thick and thin".

Basically, Debbie feels, at least at the present time, that her current friends will continue to be her friends for life.

Jobs and Careers

Jobs seem to be a common subject in dreams...and nightmares. Many people even lose sleep while contemplating whether or not they should change careers and take a risk, or stick with their current careers even though they have become boring, routine and unrewarding. Finances also are a big topic in dreams as more and more people struggle with trying to make ends meet.

The following dreams deal with jobs, careers and finances.

1. "It seems as if lately in most of my dreams, I'm in my office building and am using a treadmill. I start out walking slowly on it, but then as the dream progresses, I go faster and faster until I am too tired to continue. What does this mean?"

Grace

Although people on treadmills can do a lot of walking, they remain in the same spot and go nowhere. Grace seems to think that no matter how much time and effort she puts into her current job, she never is given any opportunity for career advancement. By the end of the day, she usually ends up feeling both exhausted and defeated.

2. "In my dream there were three elf-like creatures that appeared at the foot of my bed. Each of them told me to quit my job and spend more time at home. When I woke up, the dream had seemed so real, I actually thought the creatures were still in my bedroom."

Ava

Any small characters in dreams usually are symbolic of young children. Therefore, it's likely Ava has three children. If that's true, then her dream indicates she is feeling guilty for not spending more time at home with them.

Even though the elves were giving her advice in her dream, everything that was said came from her own subconscious, so she actually was giving the advice to herself. Apparently she believes the time has come to cut back on her working hours and enjoy more family time before her children grow up.

3. "I don't know if there is any connection, but ever since I started to work two jobs, I have had recurring dreams that all of the buttons on my shirts are missing, and all of the zippers on my jackets are broken. I hope you can shed some light on this."

Derek

Derek obviously is beginning to feel the effects of working two jobs and too many hours, making it seem nearly impossible to keep his personal or family life "pulled together."

When he heads off to work, he often feels as if he is leaving too many loose ends unresolved. He is realizing he is going to have to try to find some way to more evenly divide his work and personal life so he no longer is devoting the majority of his time to only one, while neglecting the other.

4. "In my dream, I was at my desk at work after everyone else had gone home for the day, when suddenly this figure completely dressed in black appeared and challenged me to a game of tug-of-war. I could not see any face, so I had no idea whether it was someone I knew or a stranger, but I could tell it was a male. I grabbed an end of the rope and tugged, but the other person was much stronger and I couldn't hold on."

Grant

In dreams about a tug-of-war, the person at the other end of the rope usually represents someone who has a lot of influence or "pull," commonly someone in a supervisory position.

I suspect that one of Grant's bosses has been trying to convince him to do things in a different way than he has been taught or trained to do, but Grant is opposed to the idea.

The fact that the person in the dream wasn't showing his face and was wearing all black indicates Grant considers him to be somewhat sneaky and deceitful, which could be the reason why he's resisting following any of his advice.

Because Grant did not defeat this person in the tug-of-war challenge, however, it suggests he feels as if he is fighting a losing battle against this person and therefore his resolve to stick to his own work ethics might be weakening.

5. "I dreamt I went for a job interview (I have been unemployed for nearly three months in real life) and the interviewer kept asking me what I considered to be really dumb questions, like what color socks I prefer and how many times I belch in a day. I just sat there staring at him, wondering if he was kidding."

Mark

I get the feeling Mark has reached the point where he no longer takes job interviews seriously. He feels as if they basically are just a waste of his time and no one really cares about his skills or achievements.

In his opinion, the interview's outcome still will be the same whether he discusses graduating with honors from college…or the color of his socks.

He appears to be a man who is becoming extremely frustrated with the entire job-hunting process.

6. "I dreamed I was hiking on a trail in the woods when I came across a cardboard box tied with a string. I opened the box and it was filled with about 500 $20 bills. I rushed to the nearest department store and spent all of the money on things like a new TV and electronics. But when I got to the checkout, I found out the money was counterfeit."

Jacob

It sounds as if Jacob has been considering trying some type of "get rich quick" scheme to earn some easy money without having to work for it.

His subconscious, however, is trying to tell him that if something seems too good to be true, it usually is, and the majority of fast-money plans are scams.

The string in the dream also might indicate that when it comes to receiving something for nothing, there usually are strings attached.

7. "I had a dream that I was handed my paycheck at work and the amount on it was zero dollars! I told my employer there was a mistake and he said no, that it was my new pay rate!"

Mitch

I see two possible interpretations for this dream. It could mean that Mitch is concerned he is about to lose his job and soon won't be earning any money. Or it could indicate he's thinking that the average cost of living has become so expensive, his paycheck already is gone before he even cashes it.

8. "I dreamed that I bought a pair of glasses in an expensive new style because my old ones were so

**outdated. But when I got to work and put them on, I
realized there were no lenses in them. They were
nothing but empty frames.”**

Julie

New glasses represent a desire to see something more
clearly and become better focused. Julie said her old
glasses were outdated so she upgraded them, indicating
she's trying to develop a fresh, new outlook on life.

However, having no lenses in the glasses means her
vision was impaired rather than improved.

Considering this discovery was made at her
workplace, I suspect she has been giving some serious
thought to switching to a more exciting, challenging job,
but for some reason feels as if she must remain where
she is – a place she obviously would prefer not to have
to look at or face every day.

**9. “I frequently dream I'm trying to make coffee
for my boss, Mr. Duggan, but the coffeemaker never
seems to work. It just sits there and doesn't even heat
up. I end up feeling very frustrated.”**

Margie

Coffee is associated with “waking up” someone, so it
appears Margie wants Mr. Duggan to be more alert and
aware about what's going on around him at work.

The fact that the coffee remained cold, however,
gives me the impression her boss isn't an easy person to
“warm up” to and has the tendency to be somewhat
aloof, especially when interacting with his employees.

Margie's frustration stems from his apparent inability
or unwillingness to change.

10. "This dream was really crazy, so I'm wondering if you can make any sense of it. I work in a retail store that sells men's clothing. I was folding some of the shirts and putting them on the shelf, and noticed that all of them had a picture of fish on them. I then checked the jackets on the rack and they also had fish patterns on them. In real life, the store doesn't sell anything with fish on it. And I might also mention that I'm not a fisherman!"

Roger

There are two different interpretations commonly associated with fish.

First of all, because they never close their eyes, fish can represent the dreamer's feelings of constantly being watched. Secondly, they can represent something sneaky or underhanded, as in a "fishy" situation.

So apparently Roger is feeling as if he either is being spied on in his workplace, or that some type of suspicious business is being conducted there.

11. "I have been having a recurring dream lately and am wondering what it means. In it, I'm at work and the boss asks me to get something down from a really high shelf. I get a ladder and start to climb it, but when I look up, I can't see the shelf any more, all I can see are the rungs on the ladder that seem endless, going higher and higher until I can't even see the top one at all. I always wake up before I reach any shelf."

Dalton

Dalton seems determined to make it to the top at his job, to climb the proverbial corporate ladder. His boss

59

apparently has given him the impression he has earned a much-desired promotion, yet it never seems to happen.

Despite Dalton's best efforts to reach his goal, he feels he is getting nowhere His dream will continue to recur for as long as he remains frustrated with his current position at work.

12. "I dreamed that I bought a lovely dress to wear to a dinner party my husband's boss was giving. On the way to the dinner party, however, I noticed that the dress kept getting shorter and shorter. By the time we arrived and I stepped out of the car, the dress barely covered the tops of my legs! I kept tugging it down, but it just popped right back up to the short length again. I felt really embarrassed."

Christine

I get the impression Christine is concerned that whenever she is around her husband's boss, she has the tendency to "slip up" and "reveal" something embarrassing about either herself or her husband.

The fact that her dress kept getting shorter despite her efforts to tug it back down, also indicates she usually has difficulty keeping her family's "private" matters hidden and to herself.

13. "I had a dream that a group of girls at work invited me to their 'ladies' night' Christmas party and told me to bring a gift for a gift swap. I bought a box of Florida grapefruits. When I arrived at the party, the women were acting out a scene from the musical play, 'Cats,' complete with costumes! Needless to say, I was confused."

Andrea

At first glance, this dream might sound like a bunch of random, nonsensical thoughts, but let's break it down.

First of all, in dreams, animals represent actual humans in the dreamer's life. A cat most commonly is symbolic of someone, usually a female, who acts in a catty (malicious, two-faced, spiteful) manner. So Andrea's co-workers who were wearing "Cats" costumes apparently are not, at least in her eyes, warm and caring people.

The fact that Andrea brought grapefruits, which are quite bitter in flavor, indicates she resents the way these women treat her at work. She also mentioned feeling confused, probably because she doesn't know why they treat her the way they do or how she can gain their respect.

I suspect, however, that despite Angela's obvious lack of affection for these women, she still accepts their invitations whenever they invite her somewhere because she doesn't want to cause any additional problems or friction in the workplace.

14. "I have had this dream more than once recently, ever since I was promoted to a supervisory position at work. In it, I am digging a hole in my office floor. The hole, no matter how deep I dig, doesn't come out anywhere. There is just dirt and more dirt, as if I were digging out in a garden somewhere. In every one of these dreams I just keep digging and digging. I never slow down or stop."

Jeremy

Normally dreams such as this one would mean Jeremy is taking his new supervisory position seriously and is determined to improve the business and its operation by making it his mission to dig up and uncover any "dirt" that might be hampering progress.

However, his frantic behavior (digging without stopping) leads me to suspect that in this particular situation, Jeremy might be regretting accepting the promotion at work because he feels he's now in too "deep"...in over his head.

Also, all of his digging is getting him nowhere, which could indicate he's searching for a way out of his current situation, but can't seem to find a means of escape.

Whichever the reason for his recurring dream, it's clear that Jeremy is overworked and is feeling quite a bit of stress at the present time.

15. "I had a dream that I took a break at work and went outside to sit on the bench and drink my coffee. To my surprise, I found myself standing somewhere in the middle of a huge desert. I looked in every direction but there was nothing but flat sand-covered land on all four sides, as far as the eye could see. I just stood there, not moving."

Beth

Ruling out the fact that Beth's bedroom was excessively warm while she was sleeping, which could trigger dreams about hot places, dreams about deserts most commonly represent a dry, unproductive period in the dreamer's life. They also can indicate feelings of isolation and loneliness because the landscape is so desolate.

Apparently Beth feels as if she has reached a dead end at her current job. After all, a desert is not a place where things can grow or bloom.

16. "In my dream, I was at my desk at work when I had the feeling someone was behind me. I turned around and standing there was a frightening-looking clown in full costume! I screamed, feeling scared half to death. The clown apologized, saying, 'It's me, Kevin! I didn't mean to scare you!" Kevin is a very quiet co-worker who's never upset me in any way, but all I wanted to do in my dream was get as far away from him as possible."

Sarah

Clowns conceal their true identities beneath layers of makeup and gaudy clothing. No one can tell what really lurks beneath their colorful exteriors.

In dreams, clowns commonly represent someone who has a good sense of humor and enjoys making people laugh. But Sarah's dream definitely is not about a "fun" clown because she described her co-worker, Kevin, as being a very quiet person, not the proverbial life of the party.

He appears to be someone she thought she knew fairly well, but she now is beginning to realize he is pretty much a stranger to her. For some reason, she is sensing there is a side of him that is dark and frightening...a side he apparently has been keeping hidden from her and the other employees.

Her subconscious is telling her not to let her guard down when she is around him.

17. "I dreamed that I was walking to work in the midst of a raging blizzard. I came to a street corner and the snow was so heavy, I couldn't see anything, so I had no idea when it was safe to cross. That's when I woke up."

Adam

Considering that Adam was walking to work in his dream, it most likely means his dream was career-oriented.

Snow represents a lack of warmth, so I suspect the people where he works are not especially friendly toward him. Also, a raging blizzard, or a storm of any kind, indicates turbulence or disorder in real life. So I suspect his job is causing him some problems and stress.

Being blinded means he is feeling somewhat clueless or "in the dark" about where his life is heading or what he should do about it. And having trouble crossing the street is associated with feelings of being stuck in one spot and not being able to move forward, especially in a career.

Adam seems to want to make some changes in his life, but his dream suggests he isn't certain how to go about it or how to gain a better perspective and see things more clearly.

18. "I dreamt that I was really poor and living in a homeless shelter. I remember feeling dirty and in urgent need of a bath, but I couldn't find any soap to wash with. Suddenly, my current boss in real life entered the shelter and announced he was giving away soap to anyone who needed it. Even though I really wanted to wash up, I refused to accept the soap from him."

Wendy

The fact that Wendy was dirty in her dream indicates there is something going on in her life that is making her feel bad about herself.

When her boss showed up with the soap but she refused to accept it, it led me to suspect she is doing something at work she knows would not meet his approval.

Therefore, even though her subconscious is telling her to "come clean" and confess everything to him, she apparently is afraid if she does so, she will lose her job and her source of income.

This is why she envisioned herself living in a homeless shelter.

19. "I had a dream that my boss came into my office and looked very angry. I had just popped a big wad of gum into my mouth, so when she started asking me questions about an error I'd supposedly made, my teeth stuck together and I couldn't answer her. She rolled her eyes, sighed and stormed out of the office."

Bethany

Bethany's boss obviously intimidates her. Whenever the woman confronts her, she becomes tongue-tied and the words get "stuck" in her throat, so she is unable to properly defend or explain herself.

Her dream suggests that she sees her boss as a person who isn't very friendly or approachable.

Still, if Bethany does not want to continue to be on the receiving end of this woman's wrath, she is going to have to learn how to speak up.

20. "I was wondering what this dream means. I was in a jewelry store with one of my newest employees, a young lady fresh out of college. I told her to pick out anything she wanted and I would buy it for her. She couldn't decide, so I found a silver-plated necklace with a very primitive-looking stone in it, lumpy and not polished, and told her it was perfect for her. She seemed offended when she saw my choice."

Maggie

The phrase "diamond in the rough" comes to mind, which indicates Maggie feels this employee has a long way to go before she becomes the polished, confident worker she's hoping she'll turn out to be.

The fact that the employee seemed offended by Maggie's choice of a gift, however, suggests she feels she's already a "shining" example of what an employee should be and therefore, is worth her weight in gold.

I have a strong feeling this employee is not readily going to accept Maggie's advice and/or criticism.

In Conclusion...

I hope the dreams I have analyzed in this book have helped you to more clearly understand your own dreams and the reasons why you might have certain ones at specific times in your life. I have tried to select a good cross-section of topics because so many of the dreams I receive are repetitive, but I do realize I barely have skimmed the surface of the thousands of other topics that can fill people's minds while they sleep.

Although my method of analyzing dreams might differ from those of other interpreters and "experts" on the subject, the responses I have received throughout the years have been very positive.

Sharing my knowledge always has been an extremely rewarding experience for me.

If you have any questions or comments, please feel free to contact me at sallythedreamlady@mail.com.

SWEET DREAMS!

About the Author

Sally A. Breslin (née Roberge) was born and raised in New Hampshire, where she still resides, so she is a true New Englander through and through.

She developed a passion for writing at a young age and began keeping a daily journal when she was only 12, which she has continued to do ever since. She says her journals are like having her own time machine because, for example, she can look up what she ate for breakfast or watched on TV on any given day.

Her work first was published in the 1960s when she became a stringer for a New York-based magazine called DATEBOOK, which provided her with the opportunity to interview many of the famous entertainers of that era. For over 20 years, she worked as a newspaper correspondent and photographer for a number of New Hampshire-based newspapers, covering everything from presidential primaries to local bake sales.

From 1984 –2013 she also interpreted dreams in her weekly newspaper columns, "What Do Your Dreams Mean?" and "Dreams...with Sally Breslin," which led to a regular spot on WJYY Radio as "The Dream Lady," as well as numerous other guest spots on radio shows across the country. She also was contacted by the FX Network in the early '90s and was offered a regular segment on its new morning show, "Breakfast Time," with Tom Bergeron – which she turned down because it would have required her to move to New York.

From 1994 – 2016 she wrote a weekly humor column, "My Life," which was published in six New England newspapers. In 1996, she was named the New Hampshire Press Association's columnist of the year.

She also has taught humor-writing classes for Concord Community Education.

Her short stories have been published in dozens of magazines and also in the books: "A Second Chicken Soup for the Woman's Soul," "Chicken Soup for the Soul at Christmas," "The Dog Really Did That?," and "Belly Laughs and Babies," for which she won a national humor-writing contest.

She currently writes a syndicated humor column, "Alive and Kidding," for the Senior Wire News Service in Colorado, and a local humor column, "Sally's World," for the Senior Beacon newspaper in New Hampshire.

Her humor columns, both new and archived, can be read on her blog: www.sallythedreamlady.com.

Sally's first novel, "There's a Tick in my Underwear!," which is based on her 1962 journal, is a humorous coming-of-age story about wilderness camping and young love. She also has written two suspense novels, "Heed the Predictor" and the sequel, "Conceal the Predictor," about a young woman who knows the exact date, time and way in which every person she meets will die.

Sally was married to her late husband Joe for 41 years, and currently resides out in the country with her two guard-dogs. She enjoys walking two miles every day, sci-fi movies, candlepin bowling, playing Word Whomp online and riding on old-fashioned wooden roller coasters.